a stitcher's workbook on sculptural textiles

by Fibrefusion

Nicola Bute
Susan Cranwell
Ros Dickinson
Sandra Duff
Pat Frow
Marian Harrington
Liz Marley
Madelaine Nightingale
Helen Noble
Mary Pettit
Gwen Rix
Phillippa Simons
Pauline Verrinder

Fibrefusion is Pauline Verrinder's
advanced stitched textile exhibiting group
based in Cambridge.

Introduction

Some of the best advice we have been given is "not to write a book unless we have something to say". If you were a fly on the wall at the group's workshop meetings, you would see that we always have something to say - perhaps too much sometimes. It is exciting though, to work through our ideas and challenges, to evaluate what is practical and the subject area we are most inspired by. So here we are once again, inviting you to share our enthusiasm for the three-dimensional - our fourth book, 'On Form'.

'On Form' is Fibrefusion's personal response to the experimentation with the creation of sculptural forms in the exciting and constantly evolving field of textiles.

As a textile exhibiting group we, like other textile artists, celebrate our individuality and are always amazed when sharing our ideas, at just how many different solutions we come up with in endeavouring to solve the same problem.

We don't attempt to cover every method of construction, but to offer suggestions, tips and challenges to show the way we have tackled the creation of sculptural forms, as individuals and as a group.

As with our previous books, 'On Form' is aimed at those with experience who have all the basic skills, but who want to develop the confidence to cultivate their own style

FIBREFUSION WOULD LIKE TO THANK:

HATT OWEN DESIGN
ANN FLAVIN for her fabulous cartoons
KEVIN MEAD (ART VAN GO) for his inspiring photography
VIV ARTHUR AND KEVIN MEAD OF ART VAN GO for their continuing support and friendship
OUR FAMILIES for giving us the space to indulge in our passion for textiles.

SUPPLIERS:
ART VAN GO, 1 Stevenage Road,
Knebworth, Herts, SG3 6AN. Tel. 01438 814946

Contents

1 to...form or construct

Fabrics have been formed into three-dimensional shapes since their earliest recorded uses – both to keep us warm and for functional purposes. Clothing and coverings for the head, hands and feet, together with functional items such as bags and containers, were essential items for everyday life and ultimate survival. Dexterity with stitch developed from joining two pieces of fabric together, where the creation of form using fabric became second nature, to the embellishment of fabrics for decorative purposes. This decoration often denoted power, wealth and symbolism amongst the rich and powerful.

Today, nothing is taboo - everything has artistic potential in relationship to what we can create using textiles. Most artefacts have been constructed at some time by the adventurous textile artist. Challenging items such as various sculptural pieces, vessels, installations, containers, clothing, jewellery etc.

So where do we start when we want to create a three-dimensional form?

Record and design...

Working with fabric and thread is instinctive to most of us, and we just want to jump straight into working on our project, because we 'have a vision in our head'. Is it your vision though, or is it something that you have seen in a book or an exhibition? Is it really someone else's idea? The creative experience is absent when you copy – only taking that next step and working with original source material can you truly consider yourself a creative textile artist.

To bring originality to your work, start by taking your concept or idea along the creative journey of working through the formal elements of design evaluating the many possible solutions that develop as you progress through. Every concept should have a strong design emphasis. The decisions you make from now on will depend on this.

Start off by visually recording what you see in your sketchbook – don't be frightened to use different media to record; a pencil may not be right for you – try a pen (you can't rub it out) or anything that makes a mark. You have now done the most important thing:

You have made a start...

We then work through the design development, experimentation and exploration process until we have reached that eureka moment when we have developed a firm working design for the three-dimension piece that we want to create.

Trying to work out how to construct the framework for our 3-D form can be the most difficult part of the project (see suggestions for materials and methods in the table on page 7).

Experimentation and sampling of techniques and use of fabrics follows, ensuring that originality is brought to our finished piece and most problems are sorted out.

Finally, we arrive at the long-awaited destination. We have a completed design that can be used as a pattern. Techniques have been sampled, so we can choose the most successful, but how do we construct our piece of textile art with longevity in mind?

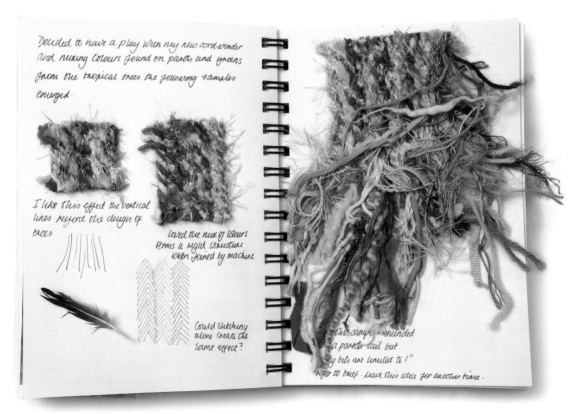

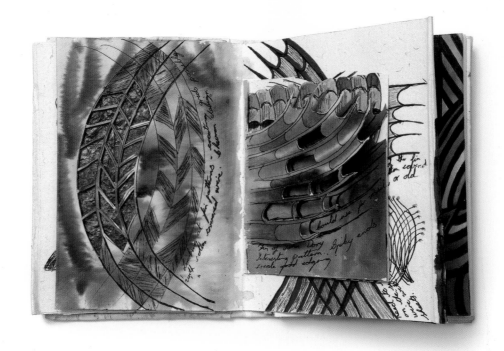

Construction

Creating any kind of three-dimensional form can often be very challenging in relationship to the materials we use, or indeed understanding how that form will hold its shape. Several things have to be taken into consideration, such as:

- How big is the item? For example, which materials should be used to enable a four foot tube to firmly stand up?
- Do you want a bowl or vessel to hold its shape, but still remain soft?
- Does the ball need to be transparent, but still hold its shape?

- Do you need to use wire or dowelling, or can you use an existing stiffened material, such as *pelmet/craft Vilene*.
- Have you a specific fabric in mind that you would like to use, but you need to use a stiffening agent to firm the fabric up?
- Can you use an existing shape i.e. a tube and build your embellished fabric around it.
- Is it a good opportunity to use recycled materials to build your form and cover with embellished fabric?

What type of materials should we try?

Techniques to stiffen fabrics construction	Firm fabrics for construction	Stiffening agents for fabrics	Framework fabrics for construction materials
Heating synthetic materials with a heat gun	Felt	PVA Glue	Wire including cotton covered wire
	Pelmet/craft Vilene	Blind stiffening spray	Boneing
Water soluble fabric (partially dissolve, leaving some of the glue-like substance in the fabric)	Buckram Paper	*Pavapol* Varnish	Card and paper Metal mesh
Heavy machine stitching	Layers of fabric	Button polish	Chicken Wire
Heavy hand stitching	*Lutradur*	Acrylic paints	Barbecue Sticks
Layering and stacking fabrics	*Permastiff*	CMC paste	Dowelling
Using the laminator to sandwich fabric and thread	Canvas	Hair lacquer	Perspex
Concertina fabrics to strengthen for construction	*Stayflex*	Starch	Plastic tubing
Plaster of Paris	Horsehair braid	Gesso	*Funky Foam*
Weaving of firm fabrics/ threads/wire	Blocking net	Resin	*Wireform*
Creating tubes	*Sinamay*	Laytex paint	Metal shim
Plaiting fabrics and threads		Slip (mixture of clay & water)	*Softsculpt*
Heat gun and melt acrylic felt or fabric		*Stiffen Stuff*	*Tyvek*
Stiffen fabric using embellisher or dry felting		*Golden GAC 400*	
Bonding helps to stiffen fabric		Nail varnish	

Construction techniques to consider?

There are many construction techniques to consider when working on a 3-D item with either fabric or paper. The following are just some of the techniques that we have tried – there are always more – but the following suggestions will give you a starting point

Stiffen fabric to hold its shape

• Stiffen fabric with Blind Spray.
• Use *Pavapol* to stiffen fabric either before or after construction. Other fabric stiffeners to look at are *Stiffen Stuff* and *Golden GAC 400*.
• Stiffen fabric with acrylic gesso. Water the gesso down by 50%.
• Paint fabric with PVA glue. Mix with 25% water.
• Stiffen fabric with diluted CMC paste or wallpaper paste diluted with twice the amount of water as usual.
• Stitch into fabric and applied to *Softsculpt* to stiffen and form.
• Stitch fabric to *Wireform* to construct.
• Use a heat gun to melt acrylic fabrics that in turn stiffens the fabric.
• If you own an embellisher, felting fibres/fabrics and threads into a base fabric will also stiffen it.

Layer fabrics to stiffen

• Stitch or bond layers of felt or fabric together.
• For a soft effect try 10 layers of muslin stitched together.
• Bond alternate layers of *pelmet/craft Vilene* and fabric together, with *Vilene* in the middle.
• Bond or stitch together a sandwich of fabric, buckram and fabric.
• Bond or stitch layers of fabric, canvas and fabric.

Manipulate for strength

Manipulating your fabric or paper will inevitably give
strength to your construction.

Try the following:

- Coiling – strips of fabric or thread can be stitched together
  to achieve a structured but soft shape.
- Roll fabric into tubes – these can then be stitched together
- Pleat your fabric.
- Create tucks in your fabric either by hand or machine
  stitch.
- Fold your fabric – try concertina style or any type of
  origami techniques.

Other techniques to consider:

- Couch wire down onto fabric either randomly, in a pattern,
  or in rows.
- Wrap wire with thread or fabric to create a mesh-like
  structure that can be moulded into a shape. The shape can
  be applied with fabric or thread. (See page 17).
- A structure can be formed with chicken wire with fabric
  wrapped or moulded around to create your form then
  embellished.
- Resin is often used to encase various embellished textiles.
- Use 'boning' to make your fabric rigid (as in corsets).
- *Stayflex* is a bondable interfacing that can be used to stiffen
  fabric.

- *Crin* (Horses Hair – sometimes called Bridal Webbing) is a
  fine stiffened braid used for stiffening in bridal wear – good
  for stiffening any kind of fabric.
- Card can be covered, wrapped or laced with fabric and
  thread – good for making fabric boxes and structures.
- Use a laminator to sandwich embellished fabric. These
  laminated sheets can then be formed together to make a
  3-D piece.

Fibrefusion challenge

Each form you choose to create may require a different method of construction, but just to help you get started we will assume that the design development process leads you to creating an embellished bowl or vessel.

Construct a bowl or vessel

It is necessary to draw conclusions from your final design. Do want your bowl to be created from a fabric that is already firm, such as *pelmet/craft Vilene*, or would it be a better effect if you used a soft fabric which you have stiffened or wired? Whichever option is chosen, you will still need to be able to embellish with stitch.

Use soft materials such as cotton, muslin and silk.

• Stiffen the fabric with a glue, such as CMC paste. The problem with this method is that if the stiffened fabric is over-handled, the tension in the fabric will be released after a while, making some areas of the fabric soft again. This can be rectified by re-stiffening after you have completed the surface design and embellishment.

• Fabric can be embellished with stitch initially and then moulded to shape with a stiffener such as *Pavapol* or even varnish.

• To stiffen a fabric, leaving it soft enough to stitch into yet still be able to be moulded, start by finding a bowl or vessel to use as a mould. Grease with *Vaseline* and then line with cling-film. Using a papier-mâché type method of layering, alternately line the mould with approx. three layers of small pieces of muslin and lens tissue/abacca tissue. Glue these layers down with a light coating of CMC paste or even wallpaper paste. The first and last layers should be fabric.

At this stage the bowl can be coloured and stitched or fabric applied.

You will probably want to stiffen the bowl further at this stage. This should be done by adding further layers of muslin and lens tissue/abacca tissue - the outside of the bowl can then be coloured. If you want to embellish the outside without spoiling the inside which is already stitched – work on a piece of coloured muslin and apply with paste to the outside of the bowl or vessel.

• Try couching cotton-covered wire over the surface of the fabric either as an element of the design OR couch the wire randomly over the fabric with hand or machine stitch making the wire an integral part of the design. The wire will enable the bowl to be formed into the required shape.

• Use the method of coiling to create soft shapes and forms. The core and working thread can be anything from wire, string, thread of any kind or even twisted strips of fabric. Using a soft fabric such as muslin builds quickly and gives a shape that can then be embellished with stitch.

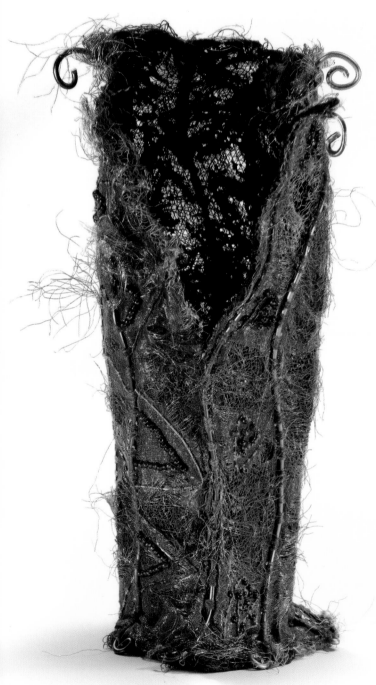

Use firm fabrics such as *pelmet/craft Vilene*, felt, boiled wool, blanket etc.,

- Colour the *Vilene* – bond with organza or other fabric for added strength on one or both sides. Stitch/embellish and construct your form.
- Cut out two or more coloured pieces of *Vilene* in a lacy design, as per the example on the front cover. Layer and stitch pieces together to give a firm structure. *Vilene* was coloured with acrylics and embellished with free machine embroidery and cords.
- Pieces of *Vilene* or felt can be rolled into a firm tube. These tubes can be formed together to create anything from vessels to jewellery. They also make good beads and buttons.
- Cut, decorate and embellish shapes from firm fabrics and piece together to create strength with the ridges and grooves. When the piecing method is used a wider variety of 3-D forms are possible. Your individual shapes could also be wired for added strength.
- Thick fabrics such as boiled wool, blanket, fleece, and hand-made felt make the most wonderful soft structures. Felt can, of course, be moulded into shape during the construction process.

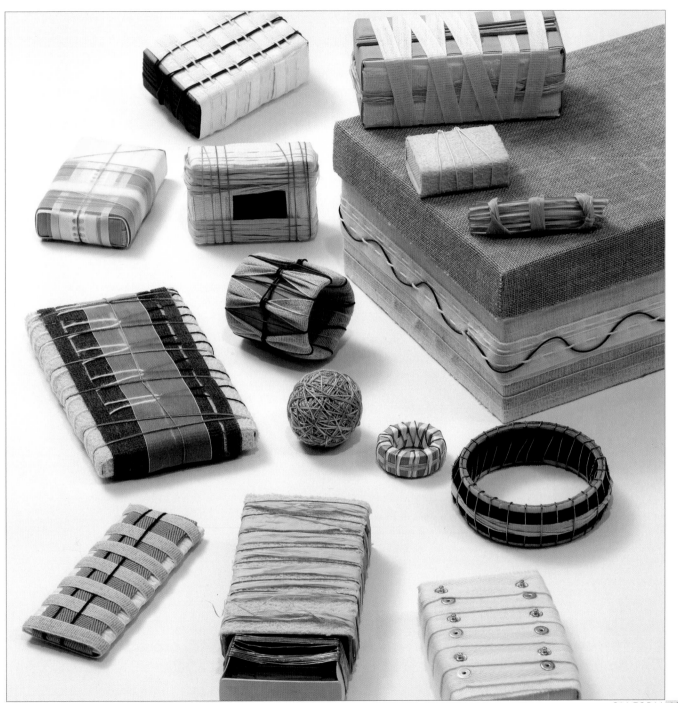

Why don't you try...

To make a vessel using the wrapped wire method

- Decide on the shape of vessel you want to construct. Perhaps you have a vase, bowl or bottle that you can use as a mould.
- We use cotton covered wire for this method as the wire can be coloured and the thread or fabric wrapped around the wire does not slip.
- If you are going to use a coloured wrapping thread, it is best to colour the cotton covering on the wire. It can be thrown in a dye bath using procion dyes if you wish, or you can quickly colour with silk paints or *Dyna-flow*.
- The wire comes in several sizes – we suggest that you use .71 or .90 depending on the size of your vessel. The thicker wire, .90, is better for the larger vessel.
- Choose either thin strips of fabric (approx. 1cm wide) – something like muslin works well, or thick cotton or silk threads. Wool isn't so successful. Some of the latest knitting threads work well.
- There are many variables that dictate the quantities of wire and thread required, so we will have to leave it down to your judgement.
- Start by laying the end of your thread down about 1cm towards the main reel of wire (1).
- Then from the end of the wire, wrap your thread evenly along the wire, covering the end of the thread (2).
- Continue to work the wrapping along the wire until you have covered approximately 5cm of wire. Coil the covered wire around to complete a circle and join by wrapping the thread over the two pieces of covered wire to secure, (3) about 4 times.

- Continue wrapping approx. another 5cm of wire, coil the wire around as per (4) and join with wrapping as before.
- Continue working with this process, creating a wrapped mesh until you have made an area of about 6cm. At this stage press the mesh around your mould to start working on the process of achieving your desired shape.
- Continue with this procedure until you have achieved your finished shape.
- Edges can be finished with wrapping or working buttonhole stitch to tidy things up.
- You can leave your vessel at this stage if you wish or embellish with stitch. The vessel on page 17 was embellished with many lengths of thread that were stretched from one edge of the vessel to the other, firmly attaching after each run. Applying fabric in pieces is another way of embellishing, leaving the mesh showing in places.
- Finally the wrapped mesh vessel can be just a way of achieving a structure that you can cover and embellish as you wish.

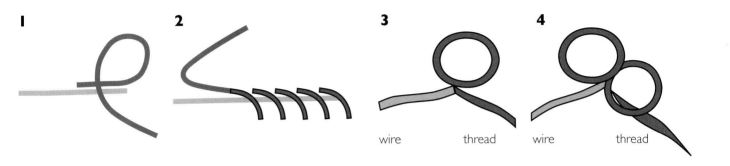

1 **2** **3** **4**

wire   thread   wire   thread

2 to...build surfaces

One of the addictive aspects of embroidery is the creation of a raised tactile surface. Building the surface using stitch and fabric is already recognised with various traditional textile techniques, such as Stumpwork, Couching, Trapunto, Italian quilting etc. How, though, can you push the boundaries with these techniques and others to elevate the surface when interpreting your design?

So where do we start?

Let your initial design exploration express your individuality and help you to focus on your vision. Reflect on the images you have created – don't just think technique – look at making marks with your fabric and stitch and interpret your design through this medium.
Experiment with ways of reproducing those marks using fabric and stitch. Try to reflect the design elements, not by stitch technique, but by considering how to reproduce 'what you see' within your design work.

Whilst attending a drawing lesson, we are told to "draw what we see, not what we think we see". It is all about good observation and the same approach applies when translating our design work and sketching into working with fabric and stitch. However, it will be *your* individual interpretation and imagination of what *you* see and *your* vision.

Build your fabric surface?

There are many ways in which you can build the surface of your fabric to create those ridges, curves, grooves and shadows that we all find so enthralling. The raised surface raises the connections between working on a flat surface and elevating a surface on a shape or form.

In the chart on the following page we suggest materials and techniques that you can experiment with to find the right path for your piece of work.

Materials (Manufactured)	Materials (Found)	Techniques
Tyvek	Nuts and bolts	• Wrap wire with thread or strips of fabric to couch and manipulate.
Fibretex	Washers	• Couch fine or coloured cotton-covered wire to edges of shape to elicit manipulation.
Xpandaprint	Tubes – rubber, cardboard	• Stitch fabric to metal shim that can then be manipulated.
Puffa-paint	Chicken wire	• Apply fabric onto Funky Foam or similar and form into a 3-D structure
Metal shim	Eyelets	• Layer fabrics – stitch, bond or both to create depth.
Wire	Old jewellery	• Create an embellished slip of fabric which can be applied onto your background and stuffed.
Cotton covered wire	Keys	• Layer fabrics together - twist and manipulate.
Wireform	Buttons/buckles	• Make stuffed fabric tubes (rouleax) – apply/ build up or manipulate.
Beads	Paper clips/ring pulls	• Pad and raise previously stitched and embellished fabrics – apply to surface.
Embossing powders		• Manipulate and apply previously stitched and embellished fabric.
Wadding		
Stuffing	See more in 'to use Recycled Materials'	Many of these techniques work well when used in conjunction with each other

Fibrefusion challenge

Fibrefusion had great fun working their own individual and experimental stitched samples building and raising the surface using 'shells' as their inspiration. As usual with these types of experiments every piece of work turned out to be new, unusual and original even though we were all working from the same bank of fabrics and threads.

On the following two pages are Fibrefusion's examples of a stitched and elevated surface. Below is a description of how each of the samples are worked:

1   *Funky Foam* shapes were couched with hand embroidery threads onto a backing fabric, then embellished with beads.

2   Raised cups were made by twisting dyed string around a couronne stick. Fabrics were then frayed and rolled with the shapes manipulated and held with wire. Buttonhole stitch using strips of material was worked around the string. Further hand stitches and French knots were used to embellish the surface.

3   Fabric was pleated, smocked, frayed and manipulated. The frayed edge was stiffened with PVA glue.

4   Stem stitch was worked onto backing fabric. Fabric was wired on reverse side to enable manipulation, then backed with *Pelmet/Craft Vilene*. Strands of thread were machined together to create bands and applied.

5   Ruched fabric was attached to backing fabric. Ridges were made by raised broken chain, then decorated with beads, straight stitch, french knots and machine embroidery.

6   Pelmet Vilene was shaped and stiffened with *Pavapol*. Strips of muslin were gathered, smocked and stitched over the *Vilene*. Spun sisal was stitched in places.

7   Frayed fabrics were rolled and formed into a shape and then embellished with wrapped wire.

8   Soft cotton and torn strips of fabric manipulated were applied to backing. Spikes were made from machining over wool and thin strips of fabric. Spikes were then applied using buttonhole stitch as embellishment.

9   Shapes were formed from painted *Pelmet Vilene* and covered in muslin. These were stitched to the background and embellished.

10 Cotton covered wire was wrapped with thread and strips of muslin and formed and coiled. The muslin was stitched and manipulated onto the base fabric and the whole piece embellished with stitch.

11 The stepped concentric circles of foam sheet were covered with fabric. They were stitched in place along circle edges. Long stitches were radiated outwards from the centre of the circle and interspersed with french knots.

12 Layers of fabric were applied onto *funky foam* shapes and wrapped with threads. The fabric was cut back and rolled.
    Couching was worked as embellishment with added beads.

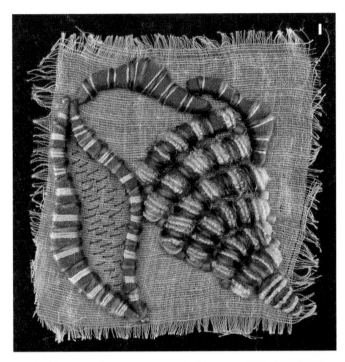

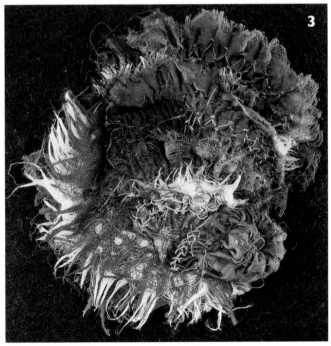

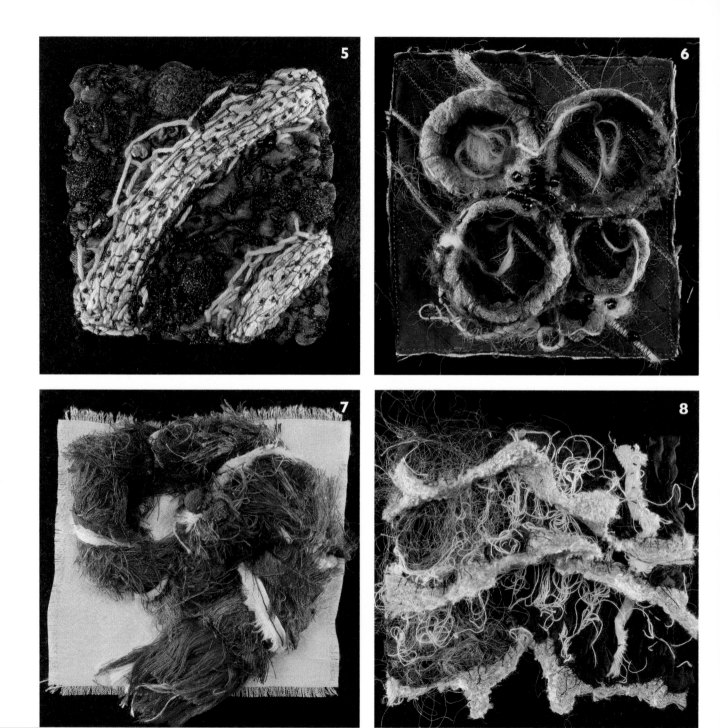

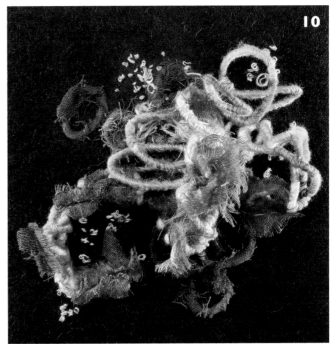

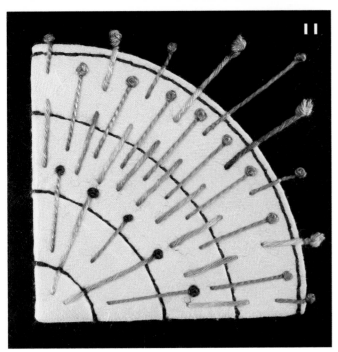

Why don't you try...

Choose your own inspiration or use shells as your starting point and work your own experimental sample trying out some of the earlier suggested ideas. You are not wasting your time - experimentation brings its own originality and energy and pushes you on to try further work. The stitched samples can always be used to embellish bags, boxes or book covers.

• You have your inspiration and have worked through the elements of design and experimentation in your sketch book. What are you trying to say? Be led by your design exploration and note-taking. What works? Determine your main shapes and focal point. Are you nearly there, but one or two elements aren't working? Hopefully your designwork invokes a colour scheme – if not, turn to your original inspiration and don't forget to look at tonal values.

• You now have a firm design to work on and are ready to start with experimentation with fabric and stitch. Your main focus will be to interpret your design and build and raise your fabric surface.

• Do you have prominent shapes as part of your design? Are your shapes solid with straight sides? if so, why not look at using card or *Pelmet Vilene* covered with fabric. Does your design dictate a smooth or textured surface? A smooth surface can be left as it is when covered with fabric. Should it need to be textured, try manipulating the fabric and embellishing with stitch, either hand or machine or both.

• Would the effect you are trying to achieve look better if you predominately used layers of fabric to build your shape.

If so, try muslin or scrim, it is soft enough to manipulate and build depth.

• Found objects, maybe covered with fabric might work – make sure that whatever you use is not too heavy and, if metal – will it rust? Tubes of card or rubber could work well. Washers, buttons, pieces of wood - try anything… that reflects your desired shape. (See Chapter 4 – Recycled Materials)

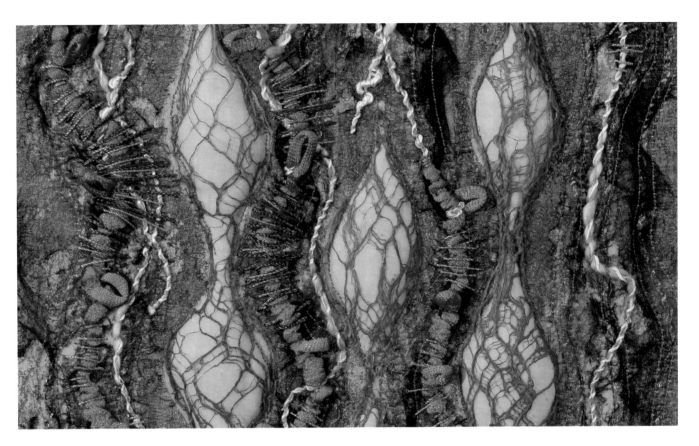

- Try a rouleau (stuffed fabric tube) or perhaps cords, if raised lines or outlining needs to be reproduced.

- Wire couched down onto your fabric will allow the shape to be manipulated immediately giving you a geometric or abstract three-dimensional form – whichever you are trying to achieve. Look also at wrapping the wire with either thread or fabric or both. Wire also gives you an interesting flexibility.

- Having manipulated your fabric, stitch can give added depth by using thick threads or working stitch upon stitch. Don't forget that you can combine hand and machine stitchery.

- Couching over threads or cords adds to the 3-D quality. Covering pipes, straws or tubes of card with fabric and embellishing with stitch all build that surface.

- Working embroidery onto a slip of fabric; applying it onto your background and stuffing it, not only elevates the surface but gives graduated edges to your worked area.

- Finally, make sure that your background is integrated into your overall design. Don't just apply a raised shape onto a plain and smooth surface (unless, of course, your design dictates that). The whole design needs to be unified with a strong focal point.

Good luck

3 to...create transparency

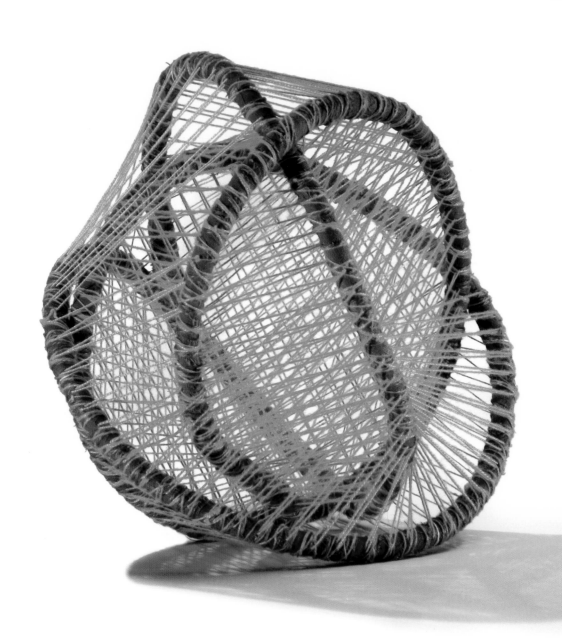

What do we mean by transparency?

An object that allows light to pass through so that we can observe what is behind it is transparent. We are not only referring to using transparent materials, but creating open and lacy surfaces when building shapes and forms.

The form on page 28 is a perfect interpretation of what we mean by transparency. Starting to create a transparent form can be a daunting project – everything is on show – there is nowhere to hide.

Points to take into consideration

• Bring originality into your work by starting off with design.
• What materials do you use to give your form the strength to stand?
• Just stiffening fabric with some form of glue or bonding agent will eventually lose its tension and collapse – we speak from experience.
• How transparent do you want your form to be? Too many holes could make it collapse, depending on the material used?
• What techniques would you use? For instance a lacy knitted piece could be transparent and it would hold its shapes if the thread was wire or a combination of thread and wire.
• Therefore, are you going to make a transparent fabric that you embellish?
• Think of the longevity of your form :
• Will it be hung?
• Will it be functional?
• If it is just decorative – how will light and dust affect it?
• Will it be constantly handled, i.e. a bag or box?
• Is it just a surround, i.e. to hold a vase?
• Take into consideration the effect that light will have on your construction. Is the location that your work is displayed important?

• Should you have the light behind it to help to show its transparency?
• Can you see through your transparent layers at all without light directed upon it?
• If it is site specific – in a commercial premises for instance - it should be fire-proofed.

Suggestions for materials to achieve transparency

Transparent materials

- Laminating plastic

- Clear plastic – can be coloured and melted to create a lacy texture*

- Plastic bags – put minimal amount of paint inside bag and small amounts of thread and snippets of fabric*

- Cling film – again make a paint and threads/fabric sandwich*

- Bubble wrap – can stuff burst bubbles – heat with heat gun or iron.

- Plastic bottles – cut and use plastic or use as a shape to work around*

- Cellophane – melt with heat gun*

- Plastic tubing – fill with fabric/thread scraps or use a syringe to fill with paint. Wrap with fabric or threads.

- Tyvek when painted, cut into holes and melted gives a lacy structure.

- Wire mesh

Framework construction materials for transparency

- Wire constructed mesh as found on pages 16 & 17 and 30.

- Wire can be used to form its own shape as shown with the abstract shape on page 28. The thick wire was wrapped with thread and used to span the open spaces.

- Wire can be used to create an armature for a doll, animal or abstract structure. Often chicken wire is used to construct the main part of a body.

- Wire can be used to couch around the edge of shapes which can then be constructed into a lacy form.

- Metal shim stitched with holes can be cut to a design.

- Wireform or wire mesh tubing can be stitched into and fabric applied onto it leaving some areas un-worked.

Transparent materials

- Plastic straws – plastic tubing.
  Perspex – melt or use to trap fabrics and threads.
  Good for framing work.

- Resin for encasing interesting embellished work.

- Sheer fabrics – organza – chiffon – nets – fruit and
  vegetable bags.

- Create a lacy fabric by making a sandwich of watersoluble
  fabric trapping threads and/or snippets of fabric. Free
  machine embroider on top.

- Construct a knitted lacy fabric – a lacy crocheted fabric –
  lace, weaving etc.

- Paper – cut to create lacy pattern –perforation.

Framework construction materials for transparency

- Use dowel and barbecue sticks to construct frames and
  shapes using wire to hold in place and be part of the open
  framework.

- Many firm plastics can be stitched into and melted to create
  lacy effects. The firmness of the plastic will be strong enough
  to hold its shape. The plastic can also be painted.
  (See page 35 and back cover).

- Firm fabrics that have already been written about in
  previous chapters can be cut into lacy patterns, stitched,
  embellished and formed into shapes. Layering the fabrics
  gives an extra dimension.

* **Always use a mask when melting plastics and
  ventilate the room well.**

Why don't you try...

- Sorry, but we are talking design again.
  What do you want to say? Use your imagination and the principles of design. What is your concept?
- You decide that you want to create a shape or form – it is to be open and the light has to pass through it i.e. you want it to be transparent.
- Using your original concept, consider the size. If it is site-specific, size may already be determined but for argument's sake, let's say that your form is a tube that will be 50cm long and a diameter of 20cm and the inspiration is leaves.

- Are the sides going to be a series of posts from which the open framework will be stretched? Or is the circumference of the tube to be solid with a fretwork of cut out shapes depicting the design?
- Choose the materials for your framework, always letting your design concept determine your choice and not a recognised technique.
- With leaves as our inspiration our decision is to keep the whole piece light, airy and fragile looking, but not glitzy.

- To depict the falling of leaves, two layers of leaves around the circumference will give depth.
- The design of a multitude of falling leaves is drawn out onto a piece of dyed muslin and the leaf shapes are outlined with couched and dyed cotton covered wire using the machine. All the leaves interconnect.
- Two pieces of fabric are stitched in this way to the measurements of the circumference of the tube. The fabric is overlapped to make it circular and is worked around the arm of the machine.

- Spaces in between the leaves are cut out, giving an openness to the work.
- The veins of the leaves are initially painted with fabric paint and highlighted with hand stitch.
- The sturdiness of the work is checked to be sure that it will hold its shape.
- A base is made with layers of Vilene covered with muslin. The two tubes are stitched by hand onto the base leaving a 2cm gap.

This is just one way to tackle a project.
Choose a stiffened fabric or just wire, and the result would be very different.

4 to...use recycled materials

The subject of recycling is very trendy at the moment, but to indulge our passion we have to spend a fortune on materials, so why not try to cut the costs with using recycled materials. It is something, that we have always done as embroiderers – fruit and vegetable bags – plastic – stripped down wire from cables – tomato paste tubes - papermaking etc.

Perhaps, though, we should be even more conscious of recycling. With this in mind Fibrefusion were given a challenge two years ago and a project was set on recycling. After an initial brainstorming session, when you wouldn't believe the ideas we come up with, some not printable – but we had some good starting points.

These are just some of our recycling suggestions:

- Paper for recycling
- Computer components
- Fastenings – buttons, zips, eyelets, hooks & eyes
- Nuts, bolts and screws
- Safety pins
- Paper clips
- Rush matting
- Blinds
- Stripped electrical cables
- Shower curtains
- Drinks cans
- Tomato paste tubes
- Wood shavings
- Tops of plastic containers

- Dried plant material
- Keys
- Swarf (filings and clippings from machinery)
- Rubber
- Hair
- Pets hair
- Tumble dryer fluff
- Balls from roll-on deodorant
- Old leather from upholstery, clothes, bags, gloves etc.
- Plastic drinks cartons
- Bandages
- Any kind of throw-away packaging
- Facial wipes
- Tumble dryer softener cloths
- Old upholstery fabrics
- Orange peel (dried)
- Chopped vegetables (dried)
- Broken glass and china
- Driftwood and waste from beach combing
- Vegetable/fruit nets
- CDs and old records
- Take-away containers
- Pond liners
- Clock and watch mechanisms
- Old glasses
- Old tights
- Hair grips
- Old clothes
- Old knitted garments
- Most kinds of plastic and tubing

Just because a book tells you that you need to have some fine copper wire to knit with, doesn't mean that you have to go out and buy some. Look in your husband's shed and see if he has some old cable that you can strip down to extract the copper wire. If it suggested that you need wool felt for a project why can't you dye old blankets.

Very often it is instinctive to have a hunt around to see what we have available at home to be able to work on a project, before we go and buy or order materials. A lot of us, when we go on holiday, take some work with us, perhaps a sketchbook, camera and embroidery that we can easily pick up and put down. Therefore, we are often restricted as to what we can use. How often do we have to improvise? Couch down found bits and pieces found on the beach. Save the plastic drinks stirring sticks from the plane and improvise making a frame from them, tied with thread or wired plastic ties because you forgot your embroidery hoop.

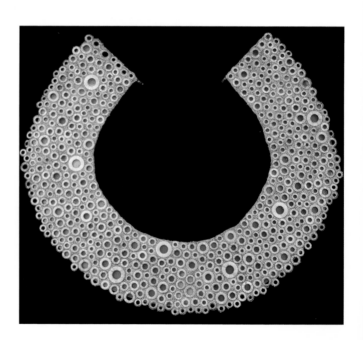

Why do we use recycled materials?

When trying to decide what makes us use recycled materials under normal circumstances – we came up with four reasons:

1 Discovering and spiriting away waste materials used in our everyday lives that we are sure we will use one day. What about old wooden cotton reels which were used in the project shown below?
2 Wanting to create a piece of art and not having the right materials (one of our children lost his camping - sleeping mat that way, and a husband couldn't find an old but beloved jumper which was accidentally felted in the washing machine).
3 Occasionally coming across something found like driftwood or dried seedheads and finding it inspirational and knowing we want to work with it.
4 Sometimes when wanting to recycle we tried hard to come up with a recycled substitute rather than purchased materials.

What to take into consideration when using recycled materials

- Is the material safe to use?
- Does it have longevity?
- Will it be strong enough to create a 3-D item.
- If metal – will it rust?
- Does it need to be cleaned?
- Can it be painted or dyed?
- Can it be melted (if appropriate)?
- Will it degrade after a period of time?
- Will the material cause marking on fabric or threads used i.e. metals can cause 'iron mould'?
- Is there a chemical content that could cause a health hazard?
- If the material is dried – is it poisonous?

Having got all of the above out of the way, there is no right or wrong way to deal with each item. Recycled materials used by the artist have to be dealt with in individual ways and much of the 'to consider list' will probably not be appropriate to your project. However, you have got your inspiration, the raw materials and the technical ability – now it has to be turned into a work of art that is brought together with good design.

That wonderful piece of driftwood is only 'wonderful' if it becomes integral to your overall design. The piece of plastic tube is only just what you wanted, if it aids the interpretation of your concept and vision and creates a unity to your finished work.

Fibrefusion challenge

When Fibrefusion were challenged to work on a recycling project it was fascinating to realise the variety of recycled materials that were used. These varied from CDs, tin, washers, laminating plastic, sweet papers, tomato puree tube, dried material and wood shavings, cotton reels, an old bicycle inner tube, stripped down cable, sugar bags, cardboard cylinders, dental floss, beachcombed rope, and old bathing hat.

What kind of forms can be constructed with recycled materials?

- Tin was formed into birds or animals.
- Laminated plastic formed into books and a transparent 3-D layered piece of textile art. (see page 35).
- Sweet papers were used to create leaves.
- Sugar bags, dental floss and an old bathing hat were used to create a tin mine.

- CDs were used to create a pendant.
- Stripped down cable used to construct an abstracted seed head.
- A bicycle inner tube was stitched into to create an abstract.
- Cotton reels were painted and wrapped to create an abstract.
- Wood shavings were used to construct a pair of Roman styled shoes.
- Glossy magazines and strips of plastic carrier bags were plaited together to create a fabric for a bag.
- Paperclips were coloured and wrapped to make a necklace.
- An embellisher was used to felt fibres into plastic sandwich bags and muslin.

The possibilities for making items from recycled materials are endless.

Our suggestions for using some recycled materials:

- Plastic can be painted, dyed in the microwave and melted (wear a mask and ventilate the room).
- Metals can be cut, stitched into, painted, pierced, and annealed. Rusty items can be used for dyeing fabric.
- Paper can be recycled into pulp for creating hand-made paper.
- Cables can be stripped down to extract copper wire.
- Tumble dryer fluff can be used for stuffing and felting.
- Balls extracted from roll-on deodorant can be dyed in microwave – wrapped with thread and used as beads or formers.
- Facial wipes and tumble dryer softening cloths will colour and can be stitched up. Some will distress with a heat gun.
- Old table cloths – the good quality ones which have a plastic type coating - are good for stitching into and will colour with silk paints and Dynaflow.
- Barbecue sticks will colour, can be couched down, wrapped with thread, fabric and wire. They can be constructed to make a frame which is wrapped with wire at the corners.
- Old tights can be stretched firmly across an embroidery hoop – organza laid on top and free machine embroidered in circular movements. When released the fabric ruches.
- Old wool jumpers can be felted. The felted fabric is wonderful to embroider on.
- Chopped vegetables such as carrots and beetroot can be chopped thinly and baked in the oven until dry and used as beads or embellishment.
- Vegetable/fruit nets have become a staple for embroiderers to stitch down, colour and melt.
- Wood shavings can be coloured, cut to shape and stitched with care.
- Drinks cans and tomato paste tubes can be cut with care and used to stitch into, colour and anneal.
- Pet's hair can be felted.
- Thick pond liner fabric is like a very thick felt and is great to stitch into.
- Driftwood can be bleached and coloured. Usually best left as it is.
- Bandage scrim dyes, distresses well and adds texture.
- Wired tubes as used with washing machines, tumble dryers etc. can be cut close to the wire, and wrapped with thread. It leaves a wonderful squiggly shape that has a life of its own. (See page 45).

'On Form' gallery

We conclude 'On Form' with a 'Gallery' of photos
illustrating some of the textile art that individuals in the
group have worked on covering the categories in the book.

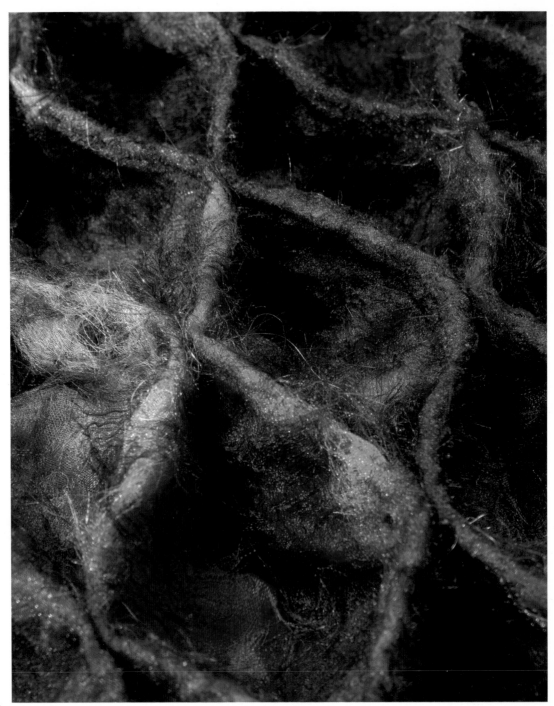